The Complete Keto Diet for Women #2019

Lose Weight, Lower Cholesterol & Reverse Diabetes| 30-Day Keto Meal Prep| Lose up to 30 Pounds in 4 Weeks

Dr Lindy Mosser

Table of contents

Introduction

It's no secret that women have different nutritional needs from men.

For one, women require fewer calories but more minerals and vitamins in their diet. Also, it's important for women to pay special attention to their intake of certain minerals specifically, iron, calcium and folic acid. A woman in pre-menopausal stage requires about 18 milligrams of iron each day. This is quite higher compared to the 8-milligram daily requirement of men.

Most of these differences can be attributed to how the woman's body is wired, and the fact that a woman gives birth and goes through other major life changing stages such as menstruation, menopause and so on.

The differences between men and women exist in weight loss as well.

Many people believe that it's easier for men to lose weight than women.

There have been stories spreading about women struggling to lose weight and doing everything they can—from dieting to exercise—but having a hard time drop a pound or two, whereas men would simply skip a meal and instantly the weight will go down.

But is this true?

Men have more lean muscle tissue than women. This lean muscle tissue is known to burn more calories than fat, even while the body is at rest. This is why, men tend to lose weight faster than women. But experts explain that this is only for the short term.

Over the long-term, losing weight is at the same pace between men and women.

Now if you are a woman who wants to lose weight, one of the best diet programs that you can try is the ketogenic diet.

This diet program actually works for both men and women.

This has been found highly effective in helping people lose weight and keep it off for a long time.

Losing weight can do many things for you. Not only will your self-confidence and self-esteem improve, you will also be healthier, have more energy and have fewer mood swings.

It can help both your mind and body, and the effect will be positive overall.

Ketogenic diet can help you jumpstart your weight loss journey.

In this eBook, you will learn everything you need to know about how to maintain a proper ketogenic diet. Included in this book are the basic information about how the diet works as well as tips for success.

Aside from this, you will also find delicious but easy to prepare ketogenic recipes that you would not find difficult to make even if you do not have the luxury of time to do kitchen work.

So, are you ready to get started?

Are you ready to start on the journey that will create a much healthier, fitter and happier you?

Then let's get onto it.

Chapter 1: Keto for Women

Why Keto?

This is the question in every dieter's mind: why should I choose to go on keto diet.

Many of them wonder: what's in it for me? Is it effective? Is it secure? Will it help me reach my goals?

Most people who have tried this diet will immediately answer a loud yes to all your questions.

However, it's important to remember that the success of this diet largely depends on you, and how you implement it. If you don't do it the right way, of course, it won't give you the results that you are looking for.

But if you do it properly, and you are consistent with your diet, it will not only effectively aid you in weight loss but it will also do wonders in improving your health.

We'll discuss the benefits in greater detail later on. But first, let's get to know what the nutritional needs of women are.

The Nutritional Needs of Women

An important thing to remember is that exercise and nutrition are the foundation of a woman's health and energy.

However, certain minerals and vitamins are necessary in various stages in a woman's life. And it's a must to know what these nutrients are so that you can choose the right foods and supplements for you.

Having the right knowledge will help you make the right choices in terms of what foods to include in your diet, and which supplements to take in.

Nutritional Requirements During Childhood and Early Teenage Years

Girls in the growing stage need to get all the nutrients they need from vegetables, fruits, whole grains, lean protein sources and low-fat dairy products.

Here are two particular nutrients that they need:

- Calcium – Calcium is especially essential during adolescence up to early adulthood when the bones are still absorbing this mineral. Experts say that girls aged through 9 to 19 need 1,300 milligrams of calcium every day. They also need vitamin D as this vitamin is necessary for the body to absorb calcium. Vitamin D intake should be at 600 IU per day for children and adults.
- Iron – Iron is needed to maintain healthy blood cells. This is very important as much as 10 percent of women in the United States and in many other parts of the world have been found to deficient in iron. In fact, up to 5 percent suffer from iron deficiency anemia, which results in poor immunity, low energy and fatigue. Girls need to take in 8 milligrams of iron each day. Once they reach 14 and up to the time, they are 18, they need to take in 15 milligrams per day.

Nutrition for Women During Childbearing Years

Once a girl starts menstruating, there is the possibility of getting pregnant.

Women who are in the childbearing years are in particular need of these nutrients:

- Folic acid – Folic acid is a form of vitamin B that prevents neural tube defects such as spina bifida in newborn babies. Fortunately, many foods are now fortified with this vitamin. During pregnancy, women are advised to take in supplements with folic acid to ensure that they are getting required daily allowance of 400 to 800 micrograms.
- Vitamin B12 – Vitamin B12, meanwhile, is important for the proper development and functioning of the nervous system. Women in their childbearing years need 2.4 micrograms of vitamin B12 each day. This increases to 2.6 micrograms during pregnancy and 2.8 micrograms during lactation.
- Choline – Choline deficiency has been linked to an increased risk in neural tube defects in babies, which is why, this nutrient is recommended for women who are

pregnant.

- Omega 3 fatty acids – Omega 3 fatty acids, which include DHA and EPA, help build healthy and functional brain and nerve cells. DHA in particular has been found effective in reducing the risk of pre-term birth. It is also known to reduce the risk of heart disease in women.

- Vitamin D – Vitamin D is needed by women not only to help their bodies absorb calcium but also to prevent skin care. Recommended amount for daily intake is 600 IU.

- Calcium – Women in their childbearing days are advised to take in calcium of between 1,000 and 1,300 milligrams per day.

- Iron – Iron also remains a necessary nutrient for women in their childbearing years. In fact, pregnant women need 27 milligrams of iron each day. Lactating women, on the other hand, only need 9 milligrams. After they stop breastfeeding, they need to increase intake again to 18 milligrams, particular once they've started to menstruate again.

Nutrition for Women During the Elderly Years

Women go through significant changes after they have stopped menstruating.

During menopause, iron requirement is reduced. However, these women need to increase intake of other nutrients because of the body's diminished ability to absorb or metabolize these nutrients.

- Calcium and Vitamin D – Bone loss, which is a common occurrence in aging women, can be slowed down with sufficient intake of calcium and vitamin D. Women between 50 and 70 need 1,200 milligrams of calcium and 600 IU of vitamin each day. Women over the age of 70 need 1,200 milligrams of calcium and 800 IU of vitamin D per day.

- Vitamin B12 – This is also another vitamin that aging women need. This can be obtained not only from supplements but also from fish, meat and other foods that are B12 fortified.

How Keto is Different from Other Diets

The ketogenic diet has become so popular that many people try to compare it with other types of diet.

It is typically compared to other low-carb diets such as Atkins Diet.

But what makes it different?

Keto Diet vs. Atkins Diet

Before we discuss the difference between the two, let us first look at their similarities.

Experts confirm that both are effective in helping people lose weight when followed strictly.

Another key similarity is that both diet programs don't require you to count calories. You only need to track the carbs that you're consuming.

People who follow either Keto or Atkins diet typically undergo minor side effects such as fatigue and dizziness. But once the body has adjusted, the side effects tend to go away on their own.

As for the differences, the primary element that distinguishes Keto from Atkins is the amount of protein that you can consume. With the Atkins diet program, there is no limit to the protein that you can take in. But with the Keto diet, you are limited to protein that is only 20 percent of your daily caloric intake.

It's also important to note that the key element to the success of the keto diet is making sure that the body goes through the process of ketosis. This is during the entire duration of the diet program. But in the Atkins diet, ketosis only occurs during the first two phases. Carbs are eventually reintroduced in the Atkins diet. In Keto diet, carbs are limited as long as you're undergoing the diet.

Keto Diet vs. Mediterranean Diet

The Mediterranean diet is a diet program based on the diet of people who live in

Mediterranean countries, with focus on olive oil, healthy fats, whole grains, leafy vegetables and legumes.

The primary difference between these two diets is the type of fats consumed.

In the Mediterranean diet, you are only allowed to consume healthy types of fats like olive oil, avocado oil, and so on. But with the ketogenic diet, you are free to eat whatever type of fat you like. Some types of fatty foods that are not encouraged in the Mediterranean diet like bacon and butter are acceptable with the ketogenic diet.

Keto Diet vs. Paleo Diet

The Paleo diet is a type of weight loss diet program that focuses on the consumption of high protein, fiber rich and low carb foods.

It pays special attention on lean meat, fruits and vegetables~particularly any food that ancestor during the Paleolithic era consumed, hence the name.

Proponents believe that by consuming the same foods that our ancestors did, you can restore your body back to optimal health, which our ancestors had at that time.

It's easy to see that the main difference between Paleo and Keto is that the former only allows the consumption of natural foods. Anything processed is off-limits. This includes even healthy grains like whole wheat bread.

With the keto diet, there is also emphasis on whole foods, fruits and vegetables but processed foods are allowed as long as these are low in carbohydrates and are within the protein limit are allowed.

How Does the Ketogenic Diet Work?

The simplest way to define the ketogenic diet is that it is a high-fat, low carb, adequate protein diet that aims to help you lose weight.

It's surprising to know however that when it was first developed, its primary purpose was not to help people lose weight but to treat epilepsy in children who were resistant to medications. In fact, it is still used as epilepsy treatment up to now.

The main process by how it works is that it puts the body in the state of ketosis.

As you know, the body burns carbohydrates for energy. Now, when you limit the amount of carbs that you take in, the body will look for something else to burn, which in this case would be your stored fat. During this process, the body will create molecules that are called ketones. The ketones are used by the body as fuel.

In the ketogenic diet, you have to get 75 percent of your calories from fat, 20 percent from protein and only 5 percent from carbohydrates. This means that you can only consume between 30 and 50 grams of carbohydrates each day.

How to Know When You Are in Ketosis

So how do you know when the body is already in the state of ketosis?

Here's a quick list of the common signs of ketosis, some of which are not that pleasant.

1 - Bad breath

People who undergo the ketogenic diet often complain about having bad breath once they have reached the state of ketosis. This is primarily caused by the increase in the levels of ketones, which produces acetone. This leaves your body in the urine and breath.

2 - Weight loss

Another sign that your body is in ketosis is when you've achieved weight loss. Quick weight loss is usually achieving in the first week. This means that you're losing the stored carbs as well as the water weight.

3 - Increased ketone levels in the blood

You'll also know that your body has reached ketosis when there is a decrease in the blood sugar levels and an increase in the ketone levels.

You can measure the ketone levels in your blood using a specially designed meter. The meter calculates the number of beta-hydroxybutyrate (BHB) in your blood.

If your blood ketones are within the range of 0.5 to 3.0 mmol/L, it means that your body has already reached natural ketosis.

The Health Benefits of Keto diet

Now we go to the benefits of the ketogenic diet.

Here are the reasons why undergoing this diet can be a smart decision for you.

Benefit # 1 - Helps you lose weight

One thing that you have to know is that the body works harder when it converts fat into energy than when it uses carbohydrates for the same purpose.

This is why, ketogenic diet has been found to speed up weight loss. But the difference with other diet programs is that this one requires adequate intake of protein, which is why it doesn't make you as hungry as other diets.

Benefit # 2 - Reduces acne

Many people who undergo the ketogenic diet attest that their skin health has significantly improved. This has probably something to do with the reduction in the consumption of refined carbohydrates, which are known to have negative effects on the skin health.

Benefit # 3 - Lowers risk of cancer

The keto diet has also been probed for its ability to prevent certain forms of cancer. There was one study that reported that the ketogenic diet may potentially be a good complementary treatment for cancer along with radiation and chemotherapy. This is primarily due to the fact that it causes oxidative stress on cancer cells but not on normal cells.

Benefit # 4 - Prevents heart disease

The keto diet can also help protect the heart and reduce the risk of heart disease. But this is only possible when the dieter only includes healthy fats in his/her diet. If you consume healthy fats, the keto diet can effectively increase levels of good cholesterol also known as HDL but at the same time reduced LDL or bad cholesterol.

Benefit # 5 - Protects the brain

Experts also suggest that the ketogenic diet has significant neuroprotective benefits. This means that this diet can efficiently treat and even prevent certain disorders such as Alzheimer's disease. One study revealed that the ketogenic diet improved both cognitive functioning and alertness in children.

7 Helpful Tips for the Keto Journey

To achieve success with your keto diet, here are some practical tips that you have to follow:

Tip # 1 - Lower carb consumption

Since the keto diet is a low carb diet, obviously, you need to reduce your consumption of carbohydrates. This is the key that will help you achieve ketosis.

This can be a big challenge at first especially if you are used to including carbs in your daily diet. However, you can gradually remove carbs from your diet to help your body reach the state of ketosis.

It is imperative that you limit your carb consumption to 20 to 50 net grams per day.

Tip # 2 - Consume coconut oil

Experts say that consuming coconut oil can help your body achieve natural ketosis more quickly. This is because coconut oil contains medium-chain triglycerides that are absorbed by the body rapidly and immediately converted into ketones.

Just make sure that you slowly add coconut oil to your diet to avoid side effects such as diarrhea and stomach cramps. Start by taking in only one teaspoon per day for one week. Increase intake to two tablespoons each day on the second week.

Tip # 3 - Increase physical activity

Anyone who's using the ketogenic diet should know that just like with any other weight loss diet program, diet is not effective on its own. You also need to get moving and to engage in regular exercise. The more active you are, the easier it is for your body to reach ketosis. Exercise increases ketone levels, and should therefore be included in your weight loss regimen.

Tip # 4 - Focus on consuming healthy fats

While it's true that unhealthy fats are not completely restricted in the ketogenic diet, it would still be a good idea to focus more on consuming healthy fats.

Healthy fats include avocado oil, coconut oil, olive oil, tallow and lard.

Tip # 5 - Take in sufficient amount of protein

Some keto dieters make the mistake of focusing only on the consumption of carbs and fat, forgetting about the equally important nutrient which is protein.

But in order for you to maximize the ketone levels, it is important to take in enough protein so that the liver will receive sufficient number of amino acids that the body needs to burn fat and lose weight.

Tip # 6 - Measure ketone levels

If you are not sure whether you've reached ketosis or not, you should make use of a ketone meter, which can be purchased in drugstores. There are testers that measure ketones in the breath, urine and blood. The one that measures ketones in the blood is the most accurate but also the most expensive.

Tip # 7 - Be determined and consistent

As with any other diet program, you need have both determination and consistency to achieve your goals with the ketogenic diet program. You cannot reach your weight loss objectives if you are not determined to succeed and if you are not consistent in following the diet's strict rules.

Chapter 2: Foods to Eat

Here's a list of the foods that you can eat with the ketogenic diet:
- Fish
- Seafood
- Beef
- Pork
- Lamb
- Low-carb vegetables
- Cheese
- Avocados
- Poultry
- Eggs
- Nuts and seeds
- Healthy oils (olive oil, coconut oil, avocado oil)
- Plain Greek yogurt and cottage cheese
- Berries (strawberries, blackberries, blueberries, raspberries, cherries)
- Unsweetened coffee
- Unsweetened tea
- Dark chocolate
- Cocoa powder
- Sugar alternatives (stevia)

Chapter 3: Foods to Avoid

The following are the foods that you cannot eat while you're on the ketogenic diet:

- Refined grains
- Starchy vegetables
- High-sugar fruits
- Sweetened yogurt
- Juices
- Honey
- Sugar
- Chips
- Crackers
- Baked goods (cake, pastries)

Chapter 4: FAQs

FAQ # 1 - Is the ketogenic diet safe?
Yes, the ketogenic diet is considered safe. There have been no reports of major ailments linked with the use of this type of diet.

FAQ # 2 - Who are not allowed to use the keto diet?
Although generally safe, the keto diet is not advisable for people who have medical conditions, and women who are pregnant or breastfeeding. If you have a condition or if you are taking in medications, you need to consult your doctor first before using this diet.

FAQ # 3 - What are the side effects of the keto diet?
Some of the most common side effects of the keto diet include dizziness, brain fog, fatigue, vomiting, stomach pain and nausea. Fortunately, these side effects go away after a week or two.

FAQ # 4 - Can you build muscles while on the keto diet?
Yes, the keto diet can help you build muscles while at the same time, minimizing gaining of fat.

FAQ # 5 - How long does it take to lose weight in the keto diet?
In the first week, you will notice that you will lose a few pounds, most of which are stored carbs and water weight. But significant weight loss takes place after two to three months of proper and continuous dieting.

Chapter 5: 30-Day Meal Plan

Day 1
Breakfast: Cabbage Hash Browns
Lunch: Beef and Broccoli
Dinner: Tuna Patties

Day 2
Breakfast: Ham and Cheese Egg Cups
Lunch: Baked Salmon
Dinner: Garlic Butter Steak

Day 3
Breakfast: Keto Cereal
Lunch: Pork Chops with Bacon & Mushrooms
Dinner: Shrimp Scampi

Day 4
Breakfast: Breakfast Stack
Lunch: Chicken Bowl
Dinner: Grilled Mahi with Lemon Butter Sauce

Day 5
Breakfast: Bacon and Eggs
Lunch: Tuna Salad
Dinner: Beef Stroganoff

Day 6
Breakfast: Keto Smoothie
Lunch: Lemon & Herb Chicken
Dinner: Baked Salmon

Day 7
Breakfast: Mushroom Omelette
Lunch: Crab Stuffed Bell Peppers

Dinner: Chicken and Carrots

Day 8
Breakfast: Hard Boiled Eggs with Mayonnaise
Lunch: Beef Shawarma
Dinner: Shrimp Scampi

Day 9
Breakfast: Keto Pancakes
Lunch: Buttered Cod
Dinner: Spicy Tuna Rolls

Day 10
Breakfast: Keto Coconut Porridge
Lunch: Italian Chicken
Dinner: Salmon Teriyaki

Day 11
Breakfast: Ham and Cheese Egg Cups
Lunch: Chicken Parmesan
Dinner: Fish Tacos

Day 12
Breakfast: Brussels Sprouts Hash
Lunch: Salmon with Red Curry Sauce
Dinner: Beef and Broccoli

Day 13
Breakfast: Sausage and Egg
Lunch: Pork Chops with Garlic Butter
Dinner: Lemon and Herb Chicken

Day 14
Breakfast: Taco Breakfast
Lunch: Tuna Salad

Dinner: Beef Shawarma

Day 15
Breakfast: Keto Pancakes
Lunch: Garlic Rosemary Lamb
Dinner: Baked Crispy Chicken

Day 16
Breakfast: Corned Beef and Raddish
Lunch: Pesto Shrimp with Zucchini Noodles
Dinner: Pork with Cabbage Casserole

Day 17
Breakfast: Breakfast Stack
Lunch: Grilled Tuna with Basil and Herbs
Dinner: Chicken and Avocado Salad

Day 18
Breakfast: Brussels Sprouts Hash
Lunch: Zucchini Noodles in Marinara Sauce
Dinner: Crab Cakes

Day 19
Breakfast: Keto Cereal
Lunch: Shrimp Scampi
Dinner: Lamb Chops with Herb Butter

Day 20
Breakfast: Scrambled Eggs with Basil
Lunch: Chicken Bowl
Dinner: Beef Stir Fry

Day 21
Breakfast: Egg Cups
Lunch: Tuna Salad

Dinner: Parmesan Pork Chops

Day 22
Breakfast: Fried Eggs with Kale
Lunch: Chicken and Mushroom Casserole
Dinner: Blackened Tilapia

Day 23
Breakfast: Bell Pepper Eggs
Lunch: Vegetable Medley
Dinner: Grilled Salmon with Pepper

Day 24
Breakfast: Keto Smoothie
Lunch: Chicken with Bacon & Ranch Sauce
Dinner: Meatballs with Zucchini Noodles

Day 25
Breakfast: Keto Frittata
Lunch: Lamb with Mustard Cream Sauce
Dinner: Buttered Salmon with Fresh Garden Salad

Day 26
Breakfast: Bell Pepper Eggs
Lunch: Lamb Curry
Dinner: Mozzarella Chicken

Day 27
Breakfast: Egg Cups
Lunch: Buttered Garlic Steak
Dinner: Salmon in Keto Barbecue Sauce

Day 28
Breakfast: Cabbage Hash Browns
Lunch: Garlic Zucchini Noodles

Dinner: Creamy Chicken and Mushroom

Day 29
Breakfast: Egg and Spinach
Lunch: Tuna Patties
Dinner: Lamb with Mustard Cream Sauce

Day 30
Breakfast: Breakfast Sausage
Lunch: Mozzarella Chicken
Dinner: Seafood Medley

Chapter 6: Breakfast Recipes

Keto Pancakes

Preparation Time: 5 minutes
Cooking Time: 10 minutes
Servings: 10

Ingredients:

- ½ cup almond flour
- 4 oz. cream cheese
- 4 eggs
- 1 teaspoon lemon zest
- 1 tablespoon butter

Method:

1. In a bowl, mix all the ingredients except the butter.
2. Mix until smooth.
3. In a pan over medium heat, put the butter and let it melt.
4. Pour three tablespoons of batter and cook for 2 minutes or until golden.
5. Flip the pancake and cook for another 2 minutes.
6. Repeat the same steps with the rest of the batter.

Nutritional Value:

- Calories 83
- Total Fat 7.5g
- Saturated Fat 3.8g
- Cholesterol 81mg
- Sodium 67mg
- Total Carbohydrate 0.8g
- Dietary Fiber 0.2g
- Total Sugars 0.2g
- Protein 3.4g
- Potassium 38mg

Breakfast Sausage

Preparation Time: 5 minutes
Cooking Time: 10 minutes
Servings: 3

Ingredients:

- 6 eggs
- 1 pinch red pepper flakes
- 2 tablespoons heavy cream
- 1 tablespoon butter
- 3 cheddar slices
- 6 patties sausage
- 1 avocado, sliced
- Salt and pepper to taste

Method:

1. In a bowl, beat the eggs, red pepper and cream.
2. Season with salt and pepper.
3. In a pan over medium heat, add the butter.
4. Pour one-third of the eggs into the pan.
5. Put the cheese in the middle.
6. Let sit for one minute.
7. Fold the egg to cover the cheese.
8. Do the same for the remaining cheese and eggs.
9. Serve with sausage patties and avocado.

Nutritional Value:

- Calories 540
- Total Fat 37.3g
- Saturated Fat 12.4g
- Cholesterol 357mg
- Sodium 850mg
- Total Carbohydrate 13.3g
- Dietary Fiber 6.5g
- Total Sugars 1.2g
- Protein 39.4g
- Potassium 712mg

Cabbage Hash Browns

Preparation Time: 10 minutes
Cooking Time: 15 minutes
Servings: 2

Ingredients:

- 2 eggs
- ½ teaspoon garlic powder
- Salt and pepper to taste
- 2 cups cabbage, shredded
- ¼ cup yellow onion, sliced thinly
- 1 tablespoon vegetable oil

Method:

1. In a bowl, beat the eggs and garlic powder.
2. Season with salt and pepper.
3. Add the cabbage and onion.
4. Mix well.
5. In a pan over medium heat, add the oil.
6. Divide the mixture to form four patties.
7. Cook until firm and golden.

Nutritional Value:

- Calories 149
- Total Fat 11.3g
- Saturated Fat 2.7g
- Cholesterol 164mg
- Sodium 75mg
- Total Carbohydrate 6.3g
- Dietary Fiber 2.1g
- Total Sugars 3.4g
- Protein 6.7g
- Potassium 207mg

Keto Smoothie

Preparation Time: 5 minutes
Cooking Time: 0 minute
Servings: 4

Ingredients:

- 1 ½ cups frozen strawberries
- 1 ½ cups frozen raspberries
- 1 cup frozen blackberries
- 2 cups coconut milk
- 1 cup baby spinach

Method:

1. Pulse all the ingredients in a blender.
2. Blend until smooth.
3. Divide into four cups.
4. Chill before serving.

Nutritional Value:

- Calories 408
- Total Fat 29g
- Saturated Fat 25.4g
- Cholesterol 0mg
- Sodium 25mg
- Total Carbohydrate 39.8g
- Dietary Fiber 10g
- Total Sugars 29.6g
- Protein 4.1g
- Potassium 523mg

Keto Cereal

Preparation Time: 10 minutes
Cooking Time: 25 minutes
Servings: 3

Ingredients:

- Cooking spray
- 1 cup almonds, chopped
- 1 cup walnuts, chopped
- 1 cup coconut flakes
- ¼ cup sesame seeds
- 2 tablespoons flax seeds
- 2 tablespoons chia seeds
- ½ teaspoon ground clove
- 1 ½ teaspoon ground cinnamon
- 1 teaspoon vanilla extract
- Salt to taste
- ¼ cup coconut oil
- 1 egg white

Method:

1. Preheat your oven to 350 degrees F.
2. Spray oil on your baking sheet.
3. Mix all the ingredients in a bowl except the oil and egg.
4. Beat in the egg and oil.
5. Pour mixture into the greased pan.
6. Bake for 25 minutes or until golden.
7. Stir halfway through.
8. Let cool before serving.

Nutritional Value:

- Calories 814
- Total Fat 76.1g
- Saturated Fat 27.4g
- Cholesterol 0mg
- Sodium 72mg
- Total Carbohydrate 21.7g
- Dietary Fiber 13.6g
- Total Sugars 3.8g
- Protein 22.4g
- Potassium 680mg

Breakfast Cups

Preparation Time: 15 minutes
Cooking Time: 25 minutes
Servings: 12

Ingredients:

- 2 lb. ground pork
- Salt and pepper to taste
- 2 cloves garlic, chopped
- 1 tablespoon fresh thyme, chopped
- ½ teaspoon paprika
- ½ teaspoon ground cumin
- 2 ½ cups fresh spinach, chopped
- 1 cup white cheddar, shredded
- 12 eggs
- 1 tablespoon fresh chives, chopped

Method:

1. Preheat your oven to 400 degrees F.
2. In a bowl, mix the ground pork, salt, pepper, garlic, thyme, paprika and cumin.
3. Add a handful of the mixture to a muffin tin.
4. Press the sides to form a cup.
5. Add spinach and cheddar in each cup.
6. Crack one egg each on top.
7. Bake in the oven for 25 minutes.
8. Garnish with chives.

Nutritional Value:

- Calories 184
- Total Fat 7.8g
- Saturated Fat 2.8g
- Cholesterol 221mg
- Sodium 125mg
- Total Carbohydrate 1.1g
- Dietary Fiber 0.3g
- Total Sugars 0.4g
- Protein 26.2g
- Potassium 423mg

Bell Pepper Eggs

Preparation Time: 5 minutes
Cooking Time: 15 minutes
Servings: 3

Ingredients:

- Cooking spray
- 1 large bell pepper, sliced into 6 rings
- 6 eggs
- Salt and pepper to taste
- 2 tablespoons fresh parsley, chopped

Method:

1. Put your pan over medium heat.
2. Spray oil into the pan.
3. Sauté bell pepper rings for two minutes.
4. Crack an egg in the middle of each bell pepper ring.
5. Season with salt and pepper.
6. Cook for 2 minutes.
7. Garnish with parsley.

Nutritional Value:

- *Calories 141*
- *Total Fat 9.1g*
- *Saturated Fat 2.8g*
- *Cholesterol 327mg*
- *Sodium 126mg*
- *Total Carbohydrate 3.9g*
- *Dietary Fiber 0.6g*
- *Total Sugars 2.7g*
- *Protein 11.6g*
- *Potassium 207mg*

Egg Cups

Preparation Time: 10 minutes
Cooking Time: 30 minutes
Servings: 12

Ingredients:

- Cooking spray
- 2 zucchinis, peeled and sliced into strips
- ¼ lb. ham, sliced into bits
- ½ cup cherry tomatoes, sliced into wedges
- 8 eggs
- ½ cup heavy cream
- Salt and pepper to taste
- ½ teaspoon dried oregano
- 1 cup cheddar cheese, shredded

Method:

1. Preheat your oven to 400 degrees F.
2. Spray oil on a muffin tin.
3. Line the muffin tin with the zucchini strips, forming a crust.
4. Add tomatoes and ham inside each of the crusts.
5. In a bowl, mix the rest of the ingredients except the cheese.
6. Pour the mixture inside the crusts.
7. Top with the shredded cheese.
8. Bake for 30 minutes.

Nutritional Value:

- *Calories 120*
- *Total Fat 8.8g*
- *Saturated Fat 4.4g*
- *Cholesterol 131mg*
- *Sodium 228mg*
- *Total Carbohydrate 2.3g*
- *Dietary Fiber 0.6g*
- *Total Sugars 1.1g*
- *Protein 8.2g*
- *Potassium 184mg*

Brussels Sprouts Hash

Preparation Time: 10 minutes
Cooking Time: 30 minutes
Servings: 4

Ingredients:

- 6 slices bacon, sliced into small pieces
- ½ onion, chopped
- 1 lb. Brussels sprouts, sliced into wedges
- ¼ teaspoon red pepper flakes, crushed
- Salt and pepper to taste
- 2 tablespoons water
- 2 cloves garlic, minced
- 4 eggs

Method:

1. In a pan over medium heat, fry the bacon until golden and crispy.
2. Put the bacon on a plate.
3. Add the onion and Brussels sprouts to the pan.
4. Sauté in the bacon fat.
5. Season with the red pepper, salt and pepper.
6. Add water and cook for 5 minutes.
7. Add garlic and cook for 1 minute.
8. Create four holes in the hash.
9. Crack one egg into each of the holes.
10. Cover the pan with its lid and cook for 5 minutes.
11. Sprinkle bacon bits on top before serving.

Nutritional Value:

- Calories 274
- Total Fat 16.7g
- Saturated Fat 5.4g
- Cholesterol 195mg
- Sodium 749mg
- Total Carbohydrate 12.9g
- Total Sugars 3.4g
- Protein 20.2g

Bacon Avocado Bombs

Preparation Time: 10 minutes
Cooking Time: 10 minutes
Servings: 4

Ingredients:

- 2 avocados, peeled, sliced and pitted
- 1/3 cup cheddar, shredded
- 8 slices bacon

Method:

1. Preheat your broiler.
2. Cover a baking sheet with foil.
3. Stuff the avocado with cheese and wrap with bacon.
4. Place on the baking sheet and broil for 5 minutes per side.
5. Slice in half and serve right away.

Nutritional Value:

- *Calories 427*
- *Total Fat 36.1g*
- *Saturated Fat 9.8g*
- *Cholesterol 44mg*
- *Sodium 941mg*
- *Total Carbohydrate 9.4g*
- *Dietary Fiber 6.7g*
- *Total Sugars 0.6g*
- *Protein 18.3g*
- *Potassium 708mg*

Ham & Cheese Egg Cups

Preparation Time: 5 minutes
Cooking Time: 20 minutes
Servings: 12

Ingredients:

- Cooking spray
- 12 slices ham
- 1 cup cheddar cheese, shredded
- 12 eggs
- Salt and pepper to taste
- Fresh parsley, chopped

Method:

1. Preheat your oven to 400 degrees F.
2. Spray oil into the muffin tin.
3. Line the muffin tin with ham and cheese.
4. Crack egg into each cup.
5. Season with salt and pepper.
6. Bake for 15 minutes.
7. Sprinkle parsley on top.

Nutritional Value:

- *Calories 147*
- *% Daily Value**
- *Total Fat 10g 13%*
- *Saturated Fat 4.2g 21%*
- *Cholesterol 190mg 63%*
- *Sodium 485mg 21%*
- *Total Carbohydrate 1.6g 1%*
- *Dietary Fiber 0.4g 1%*
- *Total Sugars 0.4g*
- *Protein 12.6g*
- *Vitamin D 17mcg 83%*
- *Calcium 98mg 8%*
- *Iron 1mg 7%*
- *Potassium 150mg*

Breakfast Stack

Preparation Time: 20 minutes
Cooking Time: 10 minutes
Servings: 3

Ingredients:

- Cooking spray
- 3 breakfast sausage patties
- 1 avocado, mashed
- Salt and pepper to taste
- 3 eggs
- Chopped fresh chives

Method:

1. Cook the sausage according to package instructions.
2. Place mashed avocado on top of the sausage.
3. Season with salt and pepper.
4. Grease your skillet with cooking spray.
5. Cook the eggs.
6. Stack the egg on top of the sausage and avocado.
7. Garnish with the chopped chives.

Nutritional Value:

- *Calories 282*
- *Total Fat 20.6g*
- *Saturated Fat 4.6g*
- *Cholesterol 164mg*
- *Sodium 326mg*
- *Total Carbohydrate 9.2g*
- *Dietary Fiber 5.5g*
- *Total Sugars 0.7g*
- *Protein 16.8g*
- *Potassium 507mg*

Chapter 7: Appetizer and Snack Recipes

Bacon Appetizers

Preparation Time: 15 minutes
Cooking Time: 2 hours
Servings: 6

Ingredients:

- 1 pack keto crackers
- ¾ cup Parmesan cheese, grated
- 1 lb. bacon, sliced thinly

Method:

1. Preheat your oven to 250 degrees F.
2. Arrange the crackers on a baking sheet.
3. Sprinkle cheese on top of each cracker.
4. Wrap each cracker with the bacon.
5. Bake in the oven for 2 hours.

Nutritional Value:

- Calories 440
- Total Fat 33.4g
- Saturated Fat 11g
- Cholesterol 86mg
- Sodium 1813mg
- Total Carbohydrate 3.7g
- Dietary Fiber 0.1g
- Total Sugars 0.1g
- Protein 29.4g
- Potassium 432mg

Antipasti Skewers

Preparation Time: 10 minutes
Cooking Time: 0 minute
Servings: 6

Ingredients:

- 6 small mozzarella balls
- 1 tablespoon olive oil
- Salt to taste
- 1/8 teaspoon dried oregano
- 2 roasted yellow peppers, sliced into strips and rolled
- 6 cherry tomatoes
- 6 green olives, pitted
- 6 Kalamata olives, pitted
- 2 artichoke hearts, sliced into wedges
- 6 slices salami, rolled
- 6 leaves fresh basil

Method:

1. Toss the mozzarella balls in olive oil.
2. Season with salt and oregano.
3. Thread the mozzarella balls and the rest of the ingredients into skewers.
4. Serve in a platter.

Nutritional Value:

- Calories 180
- Total Fat 11.8g
- Saturated Fat 4.5g
- Cholesterol 26mg
- Sodium 482mg
- Total Carbohydrate 11.7g
- Dietary Fiber 4.8g
- Total Sugars 4.1g
- Protein 9.2g
- Potassium 538mg

Jalapeno Poppers

Preparation Time: 30 minutes
Cooking Time: 60 minutes
Servings: 10

Ingredients:

- 5 fresh jalapenos, sliced and seeded
- 4 oz. package cream cheese
- ¼ lb. bacon, sliced in half

Method:

1. Preheat your oven to 275 degrees F.
2. Place a wire rack over your baking sheet.
3. Stuff each jalapeno with cream cheese and wrap in bacon.
4. Secure with a toothpick.
5. Place on the baking sheet.
6. Bake for 1 hour and 15 minutes.

Nutritional Value:

- Calories 103
- Total Fat 8.7g
- Saturated Fat 4.1g
- Cholesterol 25mg
- Sodium 296mg
- Total Carbohydrate 0.9g
- Dietary Fiber 0.2g
- Total Sugars 0.3g
- Protein 5.2g
- Potassium 93mg

BLT Party Bites

Preparation Time: 35 minutes
Cooking Time: 0 minute
Servings: 8

Ingredients:

- 4 oz. bacon, chopped
- 3 tablespoons panko breadcrumbs
- 1 tablespoon Parmesan cheese, grated
- 1 teaspoon mayonnaise
- 1 teaspoon lemon juice
- Salt to taste
- ½ heart Romaine lettuce, shredded
- 6 cocktail tomatoes

Method:

1. Put the bacon in a pan over medium heat.
2. Fry until crispy.
3. Transfer bacon to a plate lined with paper towel.
4. Add breadcrumbs and cook until crunchy.
5. Transfer breadcrumbs to another plate also lined with paper towel.
6. Sprinkle Parmesan cheese on top of the breadcrumbs.
7. Mix the mayonnaise, salt and lemon juice.
8. Toss the Romaine in the mayo mixture.
9. Slice each tomato on the bottom to create a flat surface so it can stand by itself.
10. Slice the top off as well.
11. Scoop out the insides of the tomatoes.
12. Stuff each tomato with the bacon, Parmesan, breadcrumbs and top with the lettuce.

Nutritional Value:

- Calories 107
- Total Fat 6.5g
- Saturated Fat 2.1g
- Cholesterol 16mg
- Sodium 360mg
- Total Carbohydrate 5.4g

- *Dietary Fiber 1.5g*
- *Total Sugars 3.3g*

- *Protein 6.5g*
- *Potassium 372mg*

Eggs Benedict Deviled Eggs

Preparation Time: 15 minutes
Cooking Time: 25 minutes
Servings: 16

Ingredients:

- 8 hardboiled eggs, sliced in half
- 1 tablespoon lemon juice
- ½ teaspoon mustard powder
- 1 pack Hollandaise sauce mix, prepared according to direction in the packaging
- 1 lb. asparagus, trimmed and steamed
- 4 oz. bacon, cooked and chopped

Method:

1. Scoop out the egg yolks.
2. Mix the egg yolks with lemon juice, mustard powder and 1/3 cup of the Hollandaise sauce.
3. Spoon the egg yolk mixture into each of the egg whites.
4. Arrange the asparagus spears on a serving plate.
5. Top with the deviled eggs.
6. Sprinkle remaining sauce and bacon on top.

Nutritional Value:

- *Calories 80*
- *Total Fat 5.3g*
- *Saturated Fat 1.7g*
- *Cholesterol 90mg*
- *Sodium 223mg*
- *Total Carbohydrate 2.1g*
- *Dietary Fiber 0.6g*
- *Total Sugars 0.7g*
- *Protein 6.2g*
- *Potassium 133mg*

Spinach Meatballs

Preparation Time: 20 minutes
Cooking Time: 30 minutes
Servings: 4

Ingredients:

- 1 cup spinach, chopped
- 1 ½ lb. ground turkey breast
- 1 onion, chopped
- 3 cloves garlic, minced
- 1 egg, beaten
- ¼ cup milk
- ¾ cup breadcrumbs
- ½ cup Parmesan cheese, grated
- Salt and pepper to taste
- 2 tablespoons butter
- 2 tablespoons keto flour
- 10 oz. Italian cheese, shredded
- ½ teaspoon nutmeg, freshly grated
- ¼ cup parsley, chopped

Method:

1. Preheat your oven to 400 degrees F.
2. Mix all the ingredients in a large bowl.
3. Form meatballs from the mixture.
4. Bake in the oven for 20 minutes.

Nutritional Value:

- Calories 374
- Total Fat 18.5g
- Saturated Fat 10g
- Cholesterol 118mg
- Sodium 396mg
- Total Carbohydrate 11.3g
- Dietary Fiber 1g
- Total Sugars 1.7g
- Protein 34.2g
- Potassium 336mg

Bacon Wrapped Asparagus

Preparation Time: 10 minutes
Cooking Time: 20 minutes
Servings: 6

Ingredients:

- 1 ½ lb. asparagus spears, sliced in half
- 6 slices bacon
- 2 tablespoons olive oil
- Salt and pepper to taste

Method:

1. Preheat your oven to 400 degrees F.
2. Wrap a handful of asparagus with bacon.
3. Secure with a toothpick.
4. Drizzle with the olive oil.
5. Season with salt and pepper.
6. Bake in the oven for 20 minutes or until bacon is crispy.

Nutritional Value:

- Calories 166
- Total Fat 12.8g
- Saturated Fat 3.3g
- Cholesterol 21mg
- Sodium 441mg
- Total Carbohydrate 4.7g
- Dietary Fiber 2.4g
- Total Sugars 2.1g
- Protein 9.5g
- Potassium 337mg

Kale Chips

Preparation Time: 5 minutes
Cooking Time: 12 minutes
Servings: 2

Ingredients:

- 1 bunch kale, removed from the stems
- 2 tablespoons extra virgin olive oil
- 1 tablespoon garlic salt

Method:

1. Preheat your oven to 350 degrees F.
2. Coat the kale with olive oil.
3. Arrange on a baking sheet.
4. Bake for 12 minutes.
5. Sprinkle with garlic salt.

Nutritional Value:

- Calories 100
- % Daily Value*
- Total Fat 7g 9%
- Saturated Fat 1g 5%
- Cholesterol 0mg 0%
- Sodium 30mg 1%
- Total Carbohydrate 8.5g 3%
- Dietary Fiber 1.2g 4%
- Total Sugars 0.5g
- Protein 2.4g
- Vitamin D 0mcg 0%
- Calcium 92mg 7%
- Iron 1mg 6%
- Potassium 352mg

Bacon, Mozzarella & Avocado

Preparation Time: 15 minutes
Cooking Time: 15 minutes
Servings: 2

Ingredients:

- 3 slices bacon
- 1 cup mozzarella cheese, shredded
- 6 eggs, beaten
- 2 tablespoons butter
- ½ avocado
- 1 oz. cheddar cheese, shredded
- Salt and pepper to taste

Method:

1. Fry the bacon in a pan until crispy.
2. Transfer to a plate and set aside.
3. Place the mozzarella cheese the pan and cook until the edges have browned.
4. Cook the eggs in butter.
5. Stuff mozzarella with scrambled eggs, bacon and mashed avocado.
6. Sprinkle cheese on top.
7. Season with salt and pepper.

Nutritional Value:

- *Calories 645*
- *Total Fat 53.6g*
- *Saturated Fat 21.9g*
- *Cholesterol 575mg*
- *Sodium 1101mg*
- *Total Carbohydrate 6.5g*
- *Dietary Fiber 3.4g*
- *Total Sugars 1.4g*
- *Protein 35.8g*
- *Potassium 600mg*

Keto Cheese Chips

Preparation Time: 10 minutes
Cooking Time: 10 minutes
Servings: 3

Ingredients:

- 1 ½ cups cheddar cheese, shredded
- 3 tablespoons ground flaxseed meal
- Garlic salt to taste

Method:

1. Preheat your oven to 425 degrees F.
2. Create a small pile of 2 tablespoons cheddar cheese on a baking sheet.
3. Sprinkle flaxseed on top of each chip.
4. Season with garlic salt.
5. Bake in the oven for 10 minutes.
6. Let cool before serving.

Nutritional Value:

- Calories 288
- Total Fat 22.2g
- Saturated Fat 11.9g
- Cholesterol 59mg
- Sodium 356mg
- Total Carbohydrate 5.8g
- Dietary Fiber 4g
- Total Sugars 0.3g
- Protein 17.1g
- Potassium 57mg

Chapter 8: Beef, Pork and Lamb Recipes

Beef & Broccoli

Preparation Time: 10 minutes
Cooking Time: 15 minutes
Servings: 2

Ingredients:

- ¼ cup coconut amino, divided
- 1 teaspoon garlic, minced and divided
- 1 teaspoon fresh ginger, minced and divided
- 8 oz. beef, sliced thinly
- 1 ½ tablespoon avocado oil, divided
- 2 ½ cups broccoli, sliced into florets
- ¼ cup low sodium beef stock
- ½ teaspoon sesame oil
- Salt to taste
- Sesame seeds
- Green onion, chopped

Method:

1. In a bowl, mix the one tablespoon coconut amino with half of the ginger and garlic.
2. Marinate the beef into this mixture for 1 hour.
3. Cover with foil and place in the refrigerator.
4. Put 1 tablespoon oil in a pan over medium heat.
5. Add the broccoli and cook for 3 minutes.
6. Add the remaining ginger and garlic.
7. Cook for 1 minute.
8. Reduce the heat.
9. Cover the pan with its lid.
10. Cook until the broccoli is tender but still a little crunchy.
11. Transfer the broccoli to a platter.
12. Increase the heat and add the remaining oil.
13. Add the beef and cook for 3 minutes.

14. Put the broccoli back.
15. In a bowl, mix the remaining coconut amino, broth and sesame oil.
16. Pour into the pan.
17. Cook until the sauce has thickened.
18. Season with salt.
19. Garnish with sesame seeds and green onion.

Nutritional Value:

- *Calories 298*
- *Total Fat 10g*
- *Saturated Fat 3.1g*
- *Cholesterol 101mg*
- *Sodium 1989mg*

- *Total Carbohydrate 12.2g*
- *Dietary Fiber 4g*
- *Total Sugars 2.7g*
- *Protein 40g*
- *Potassium 958mg*

Beef Stroganoff

Preparation Time: 20 minutes
Cooking Time: 2 hours and 10 minutes
Servings: 10

Ingredients:

- ¼ cup avocado oil
- 1 white onion, chopped
- 2 teaspoons garlic, minced
- 3 lb. beef brisket, fat trimmed and sliced into bite size pieces
- Salt and pepper to taste
- 2 teaspoons ground thyme
- 1 ½ cups beef broth
- 2 tablespoons apple cider vinegar
- 16 oz. fresh mushrooms, sliced
- ¾ cup sour cream
- ¼ cup mayonnaise
- 1 ½ teaspoon xanthan gum

Method:

1. Place your pan over medium heat.
2. Add the oil, onion and garlic.
3. Sauté for 3 minutes.
4. Add the beef.
5. Season with salt, pepper and thyme.
6. Cook for 8 minutes, stirring frequently.
7. Reduce heat and add beef broth and vinegar.
8. Simmer for 30 minutes.
9. Add mushrooms and cover the pan.
10. Simmer for 1 hour and 30 minutes.
11. Remove the pan from the stove.
12. Stir in the mayonnaise and sour cream.
13. Gradually stir in the xanthan gum until the sauce has thickened.
14. Cover the pan and let sit for 10 minutes before serving.

Nutritional Value:

- *Calories 343*
- *Total Fat 15.1g*

- *Saturated Fat 6g*
- *Cholesterol 131mg*
- *Sodium 292mg*
- *Total Carbohydrate 6.5g*

- *Dietary Fiber 2g*
- *Total Sugars 1.8g*
- *Protein 44.4g*
- *Potassium 789mg*

Garlic Butter Steak

Preparation Time: 10 minutes
Cooking Time: 15 minutes
Servings: 2

Ingredients:

- 2 rib eye steaks, trimmed
- 1 ½ tablespoons olive oil, divided
- Salt and pepper to taste
- 2 tablespoons butter
- 2 cloves garlic, minced
- 2 sprigs fresh rosemary, chopped

Method:

1. Dry the steaks using a paper towel.
2. Put a cast iron skillet over high heat.
3. Wait until the skillet starts to smoke.
4. Add 1 tablespoon oil to the skillet.
5. Coat the steaks with the remaining oil.
6. Season steaks with salt and pepper.
7. Add the steaks to the hot pan.
8. Sear for 5 to 7 minutes for medium and up to 10 minutes for medium well.
9. Reduce the heat to low.
10. Add the butter, garlic and the rosemary.
11. Cook for another minute.
12. Let the steak rest for before slicing and serving.

Nutritional Value:

- Calories 547
- Total Fat 48.1g
- Saturated Fat 19.3g
- Cholesterol 120mg
- Sodium 142mg
- Total Carbohydrate 1.2g
- Dietary Fiber 0.4g
- Total Sugars 0g
- Protein 26.9g
- Potassium 18mg

Beef Shawarma

Preparation Time: 5 minutes
Cooking Time: 15 minutes
Servings: 4

Ingredients:

- 2 tablespoons olive oil
- 1 lb. lean ground beef
- 1 cup onion, sliced
- Salt to taste
- 3 tablespoons shawarma mix
- 3 cups cabbage, shredded
- 2 tablespoons water
- 1/4 cup parsley, chopped

Method:

1. Put your pan over medium heat.
2. Once the pan starts to sizzle, add the olive oil.
3. Add the ground beef.
4. Add the onion and cook for 4 minutes.
5. Season with salt and shawarma mix.
6. Add the cabbage.
7. Pour in the water.
8. Cover the pan and steam for 1 minute.
9. Garnish with parsley before serving.

Nutritional Value:

- Calories 330
- Total Fat 15.3g
- Saturated Fat 4.1g
- Cholesterol 101mg
- Sodium 201mg
- Total Carbohydrate 12g
- Dietary Fiber 4.3g
- Total Sugars 2.9g
- Protein 35.9g
- Potassium 609mg

Pork Chops with Bacon & Mushrooms

Preparation Time: 10 minutes
Cooking Time: 20 minutes
Servings: 4

Ingredients:

- 6 strips bacon, chopped
- 4 pork chops
- Salt and pepper to taste
- 2 cloves garlic, minced
- 8 oz. mushrooms, sliced
- 1 tablespoon olive oil
- 5 sprigs fresh thyme
- 2/3 cup chicken broth
- 1/2 cup heavy cream

Method:

1. Cook bacon in a pan until crispy.
2. Transfer bacon on a plate.
3. Sprinkle salt and pepper on the pork chops.
4. Cook the pork chops in bacon fat for 4 minutes per side.
5. Transfer pork chops on a plate.
6. Add the garlic and mushrooms in the pan.
7. Add the olive oil
8. Cook for 5 minutes.
9. Pour in the broth and let the mixture boil.
10. Stir in the heavy cream and reduce the heat to low.
11. Put the bacon and pork chops back to the pan.
12. Cook for 3 more minutes before serving.

Nutritional Value:

- *Calories 516*
- *Total Fat 41.3g*
- *Saturated Fat 15.4g*
- *Cholesterol 121mg*
- *Sodium 851mg*
- *Total Carbohydrate 4.2g*
- *Dietary Fiber 1.1g*
- *Total Sugars 1.2g*
- *Protein 31.7g*
- *Potassium 679mg*

Pork with Cabbage Casserole

Preparation Time: 15 minutes
Cooking Time: 1 hour
Servings: 4

Ingredients:

- 2 tablespoons olive oil
- 1 onion, chopped
- 2 cloves garlic, minced
- 2 lb. green cabbage, chopped
- ½ cup sour cream
- 1¼ cups heavy whipping cream
- 5 oz. cream cheese
- Salt and pepper to taste
- 1 tablespoon ranch seasoning
- 5 oz. shredded cheese
- 2 lb. pork chops
- 3 tablespoons butter

Method:

1. Preheat your oven to 400 degrees F.
2. Add the olive oil the pan and sauté the onion, garlic and cabbage for 10 minutes.
3. Add the sour cream, heavy cream and cream cheese.
4. Season with salt, pepper and ranch seasoning.
5. Simmer for 10 minutes.
6. Transfer to a baking dish.
7. Add the cheese on top.
8. Bake in the oven for 20 minutes.
9. Season the pork chops with salt and pepper.
10. Fry in the pan on butter until cooked on both sides.
11. Serve the pork chops with the cabbage casserole.

Nutritional Value:

- Calories 760
- Total Fat 65g
- Saturated Fat 31.9g
- Cholesterol 206mg
- Sodium 321mg
- Total Carbohydrate 10.6g
- Dietary Fiber 3.2g
- Total Sugars 4.4g
- Protein 34.2g
- Potassium 697mg

Pork Chops with Garlic Butter

Preparation Time: 10 minutes
Cooking Time: 20 minutes
Servings: 4

Ingredients:

- 4 pork chops
- Salt and pepper to taste
- 2 oz. butter
- 1 lb. green beans

For garlic butter sauce

- 5 oz. butter
- 1 tablespoon dried parsley
- ½ tablespoons garlic powder
- 1 tablespoon lemon juice
- Salt and pepper to taste

Method:

1. Mix the ingredients for the garlic butter sauce.
2. Set aside.
3. Season the pork chops with salt and pepper.
4. Put the pan over medium high heat.
5. Add the butter.
6. Cook the pork chops in butter for 5 minutes per side.
7. Transfer the pork chops to a plate.
8. Add the beans
9. Sprinkle with salt and pepper.
10. Cook until tender but still firm.
11. Pour the garlic butter over the pork chops and beans and serve.

Nutritional Value:

- *Calories 652*
- *Total Fat 60.3g*
- *Saturated Fat 33g*
- *Cholesterol 175mg*
- *Total Carbohydrate 9g*
- *Dietary Fiber 4g*
- *Total Sugars 2g*
- *Protein 20.7g*

Parmesan Pork Chops

Preparation Time: 6 minutes
Cooking Time: 12 minutes
Servings: 4

Ingredients:

- 4 boneless pork chops
- Salt and pepper to taste
- 2 tablespoons olive oil

For Parmesan crust

- ½ cup Parmesan cheese, grated
- ½ cup pork rinds, crushed
- 1 tablespoon fresh parsley, minced
- ½ teaspoon fresh garlic, minced
- ½ teaspoon lemon zest
- 1 egg, beaten
- 2 teaspoons water

Method:

1. Pat the pork chops with paper towel to dry.
2. Season with salt and pepper. Set aside.
3. Put the egg and water in a bowl.
4. Put the Parmesan and pork rinds on a plate.
5. Add the parsley, lemon zest and garlic to the Parmesan mixture.
6. In a pan over medium heat, add the olive oil.
7. Dip the pork chop in the egg wash and dredge with the Parmesan mixture.
8. Cook until both sides of the pork chops are golden and crunchy.

Nutritional Value:

- Calories 574
- Total Fat 21.2g
- Saturated Fat 6.1g
- Cholesterol 289mg
- Sodium 272mg
- Total Carbohydrate 0.5g
- Dietary Fiber 0.1g
- Total Sugars 0.1g
- Protein 90.8g
- Potassium 1424mg

Lamb Chops with Herb Butter

Preparation Time: 10 minutes
Cooking Time: 10 minutes
Servings: 8

Ingredients:

- 8 lamb chops
- 1 tablespoon butter
- 1 tablespoon olive oil
- Salt and pepper to taste
- 4 oz. herb butter
- 1 lemon, sliced into wedges

Method:

1. Season the lamb chops with salt and pepper.
2. Fry in butter and olive oil for 3 to 4 minutes per side.
3. Pour the herb butter on top and garnish with lemon wedges before serving.

Nutritional Value:

- Calories 638
- Total Fat 27.2g
- Saturated Fat 9.7g
- Cholesterol 298mg
- Sodium 259mg
- Total Carbohydrate 0.7g
- Dietary Fiber 0.2g
- Total Sugars 0.2g
- Protein 91.9g
- Potassium 1106mg

Lamb Curry

Preparation Time: 15 minutes
Cooking Time: 1 hour and 20 minutes
Servings: 14

Ingredients:

For the marinade

- 2 teaspoons Ginger finely chopped or crushed
- 3 cloves garlic, minced
- 2 teaspoons ground cumin
- 2 teaspoons ground coriander
- 1 teaspoon onion powder
- 1 teaspoon ground cardamom
- 1 teaspoon ground paprika
- 1 teaspoon ground turmeric
- 1 teaspoon chili powder
- 2 tablespoons olive oil

For the curry

- 4 lb. lamb shoulder, diced
- 3 tablespoons ghee
- 1 onion, diced
- 1 teaspoon ground cinnamon
- 1 teaspoon chili powder
- Salt and pepper to taste
- 1 cup heavy cream
- ½ cup almonds, chopped
- 3 tablespoons cilantro, chopped

Method:

1. Mix all the ingredients for the marinade in a bowl.
2. Add the lamb and coat well.
3. Marinate in the refrigerator covered for 1 hour.
4. In a saucepan, add the ghee, onion, chili powder and cinnamon.
5. Cook for 3 minutes.
6. Add the lamb.
7. Season with salt and pepper.
8. Cook lamb for 10 minutes.
9. Add the cream and reduce the heat to low.
10. Simmer for 1 hour or until lamb is tender.

11. Add the almond and other seasonings.
12. Garnish with cilantro before serving.

Nutritional Value:

- Calories 340
- Total Fat 19.3g
- Saturated Fat 7.5g
- Cholesterol 135mg
- Sodium 107mg

- Total Carbohydrate 2.7g
- Dietary Fiber 0.9g
- Total Sugars 0.6g
- Protein 37.6g
- Potassium 503mg

Lamb with Mustard Cream Sauce

Preparation Time: 10 minutes
Cooking Time: 20 minutes
Servings: 4

Ingredients:

- 6 lamb chops
- 2 cloves garlic, minced
- 1 tablespoon fresh rosemary, minced
- 2 tablespoons olive oil
- Salt and pepper to taste

Mustard cream sauce

- 1 tablespoon shallot, minced
- ½ cup beef stock
- 2 tablespoons Brandy
- 2/3 cup heavy cream
- 1 tablespoon mustard
- 2 teaspoons lemon juice
- 2 teaspoons Worcestershire sauce
- 1 teaspoon erythritol
- 1 sprig rosemary
- 1 sprig of thyme
- 2 tablespoons butter
- Salt and pepper to taste

Method:

1. Season the lamp chops with salt and pepper.
2. Mix the garlic, olive oil and rosemary in a bowl.
3. Marinate the lamb chops in this mixture for 1 hour.
4. Fry the lamb chops until thoroughly cooked on both sides in a pan with hot oil.
5. Mix the sauce ingredients.
6. Add to the lamb chops.
7. Simmer for 10 minutes.
8. Remove herb sprigs before serving.

Nutritional Value:

- *Calories 745*
- *Total Fat 38.1g*

- Saturated Fat 14.8g
- Cholesterol 323mg
- Sodium 365mg
- Total Carbohydrate 2.4g
- Dietary Fiber 0.5g
- Total Sugars 0.5g
- Protein 93g
- Potassium 1147mg

Garlic Rosemary Lamb

Preparation Time: 30 minutes
Cooking Time: 30 minutes
Servings: 3

Ingredients:

- 3 teaspoons fresh rosemary, chopped
- 2 cloves garlic, minced
- 4 tablespoons ghee
- Salt and pepper to taste
- 6 lamb chops

Method:

1. In a bowl, add the rosemary, garlic and ghee.
2. Cover the bowl with a foil and put in the refrigerator.
3. Season the lamb with salt and pepper.
4. Grill or bake until cooked on both sides, or for up to 25 minutes.
5. Slice the ghee into small discs.
6. Add to the pork chops and put it back to the grill or oven until the ghee has melted on top of the chops.

Nutritional Value:

- Calories 686
- Total Fat 32.6g
- Saturated Fat 13.9g
- Cholesterol 316mg
- Sodium 249mg
- Total Carbohydrate 0.7g
- Dietary Fiber 0.3g
- Total Sugars 0g
- Protein 91.9g
- Potassium 1106mg

Chapter 9: Poultry Recipes

Baked Crispy Chicken

Preparation Time: 10 minutes
Cooking Time: 40 minutes
Servings: 12

Ingredients:

- 4 oz. pork rinds
- Salt and pepper to taste
- 1 teaspoon oregano
- 1 ½ teaspoons thyme
- 1 teaspoon smoke paprika
- ½ teaspoon garlic powder
- 12 chicken legs
- 2 oz. mayonnaise
- 1 egg
- 3 tablespoons Dijon mustard

Method:

1. Preheat your oven to 400 degrees F.
2. Grind pork rinds until they've turned into powdery texture.
3. Mix pork rinds with salt, pepper, oregano, thyme, paprika and garlic powder.
4. Spread mixture on a plate.
5. In a bowl, mix the mayo, egg and mustard.
6. Dip each chicken leg first into the egg mixture then coat with the pork rind mixture.
7. Bake in the oven for 40 minutes.

Nutritional Value:

- Calories 359
- Total Fat 16.3g
- Saturated Fat 4.7g
- Cholesterol 158mg
- Sodium 391mg
- Total Carbohydrate 1.6g
- Dietary Fiber 0.3g
- Total Sugars 0.4g
- Protein 49g
- Potassium 370mg

Italian Chicken

Preparation Time: 10 minutes
Cooking Time: 15 minutes
Servings: 4

Ingredients:

- 2 tablespoons olive oil
- 1 ½ lb. chicken breast meat, sliced thinly
- ½ cup chicken broth
- 1 cup heavy cream
- 1 teaspoon Italian seasoning
- ½ cup Parmesan cheese
- 1 teaspoon garlic powder
- 1 cup spinach, chopped
- ½ cup sun dried tomatoes

Method:

1. In a pan over medium heat, add olive oil.
2. Cook chicken for 4 to 5 minutes per side.
3. Transfer chicken on a plate.
4. Stir in the broth, cream, Italian seasoning, Parmesan cheese and garlic powder.
5. Simmer until the sauce has thickened.
6. Add the tomatoes and spinach.
7. Cook until the spinach has wilted.
8. Put the chicken back to the pan and serve.

Nutritional Value:

- Calories 535
- Total Fat 29.4g
- Saturated Fat 11g
- Cholesterol 199mg
- Sodium 317mg
- Total Carbohydrate 6.1g
- Dietary Fiber 1g
- Total Sugars 0.4g
- Protein 60.3g
- Potassium 783mg

Chicken & Carrots

Preparation Time: 15 minutes
Cooking Time: 20 minutes
Servings: 4

Ingredients:

- 1 ½ lb. carrots, peeled and sliced
- 1 onion, sliced into quarters
- 1 head garlic, top sliced off
- 4 tablespoons olive oil, divided
- Salt and pepper to taste
- 1 tablespoon fresh rosemary, chopped
- 4 chicken thighs

Method:

1. Preheat your oven to 425 degrees F.
2. Arrange the onion and carrots on a single layer on a baking pan.
3. Place the garlic in the middle of the tray.
4. Drizzle half of the olive oil over the vegetables.
5. Season with salt, pepper and rosemary.
6. Coat the chicken with the remaining oil.
7. Season with salt and pepper.
8. Bake in the oven for 20 minutes.

Nutritional Value:

- *Calories 532*
- *Total Fat 25.2g*
- *Saturated Fat 5.1g*
- *Cholesterol 130mg*
- *Sodium 250mg*
- *Total Carbohydrate 31.1g*
- *Dietary Fiber 5.8g*
- *Total Sugars 9.9g*
- *Protein 46.1g*
- *Potassium 1083mg*

Lemon & Herb Chicken

Preparation Time: 20 minutes
Cooking Time: 60 minutes
Servings: 6

Ingredients:

- 1 whole chicken
- 4 tablespoons unsalted butter
- 3 lemons, sliced in half
- ½ bunch thyme
- ½ bunch rosemary
- Salt and pepper to taste

Method:

1. Preheat your oven to 425 degrees F.
2. Cover the baking pan with foil.
3. Put a roasting rack on top.
4. Rub the chicken with butter.
5. Stuff the insides with lemon slices and herbs.
6. Season both inside and outside of chicken with salt and pepper.
7. Use twine to tie the chicken legs together.
8. Put the chicken on a roasting rack.
9. Roast for 40 minutes.
10. Reduce heat to 375 degrees F and roast until chicken is fully cooked.
11. Let chicken rest for 15 minutes before slicing and serving.

Nutritional Value:

- Calories 504
- Total Fat 36.1g
- Saturated Fat 15g
- Cholesterol 180mg
- Sodium 216mg
- Total Carbohydrate 4.3g
- Dietary Fiber 1.8g
- Total Sugars 0.8g
- Protein 42.6g
- Potassium 65mg

Chicken & Avocado Salad

Preparation Time: 5 minutes
Cooking Time: 15 minutes
Servings: 4

Ingredients:

Chicken

- ¼ cup water
- 2 boneless chicken thigh fillets
- 2 tablespoons olive oil
- Salt and pepper to taste
- 1 teaspoon sweet chili powder
- 1 teaspoon dried thyme
- 4 cloves garlic

Salad

- 2 cups arugula
- 1 cup purslane leaves
- 1 cup basil leaves
- ½ cup fresh dill
- ½ cup cherry tomatoes, sliced in half
- 1 tablespoon olives
- 1 avocado, sliced
- 1 teaspoon sesame seeds
- ½ tablespoon olive oil
- 2 tablespoons avocado dressing

Method:

1. Pour water into a skillet.
2. Cook chicken over medium low heat for 5 minutes.
3. Drizzle olive oil over the chicken
4. Season with the salt, pepper, thyme and chili powder.
5. Cook until golden, flipping several times to cook evenly.
6. Chop the chicken.
7. Arrange all the ingredients for the salad in a bowl.
8. Put the chicken on top of the salad.
9. Drizzle with the avocado dressing and olive oil.
10. Sprinkle sesame seeds on top.

Nutritional Value:

- Calories 517
- Total Fat 38.6g
- Saturated Fat 6.4g
- Cholesterol 70mg
- Sodium 368mg

- Total Carbohydrate 27.3g
- Dietary Fiber 9.9g
- Total Sugars 7.2g
- Protein 22g
- Potassium 1102mg

Chicken Bowl

Preparation Time: 10 minutes
Cooking Time: 20 minutes
Servings: 4

Ingredients:

- Salt and pepper to taste
- 2 teaspoons basil
- 2 teaspoon rosemary
- 2 teaspoons thyme
- 1 teaspoon paprika
- 2 lb. chicken breast meat, sliced into bite sized pieces
- 1 ½ cups broccoli florets
- 1 onion, chopped
- 1 cup tomatoes
- 1 zucchini, chopped
- 2 teaspoons garlic, minced
- 2 tablespoons olive oil
- 2 cups cauliflower rice

Method:

1. Preheat your oven to 450 degrees F.
2. Cover your baking pan with foil. Set aside.
3. In a bowl, mix salt, pepper and spices.
4. Put the chicken and vegetables on a baking pan.
5. Sprinkle the spice mixture and garlic over the vegetables and chicken.
6. Drizzle olive oil on top.
7. Bake in the oven for 20 minutes.
8. Broil the chicken for 2 minutes.
9. Serve the chicken and vegetables in a bowl on top of cauliflower rice.

Nutritional Value:

- *Calories 558*
- *Total Fat 19.1g*
- *Saturated Fat 4.4g*
- *Cholesterol 206mg*
- *Sodium 260mg*
- *Total Carbohydrate 14.2g*
- *Dietary Fiber 3.3g*
- *Total Sugars 5.9g*
- *Protein 80.3g*
- *Potassium 1039mg*

Chicken with Bacon & Ranch Sauce

Preparation Time: 10 minutes
Cooking Time: 20 minutes
Servings: 4

Ingredients:

- 4 chicken breasts
- 1 teaspoon paprika
- 1 teaspoon garlic powder
- 1 teaspoon onion powder
- 1 tablespoon avocado oil
- 6 oz. cream cheese
- 1 tablespoon ranch seasoning powder
- 1 cup cheddar, grated
- 10 slices bacon, cooked and crumbled
- 2 tablespoons green onions, chopped

Method:

1. Preheat your oven to 375 degrees F.
2. Season the chicken with the paprika, garlic powder and onion powder.
3. Pour the oil in a pan over medium heat.
4. Cook the chicken in a pan over medium heat.
5. Cook for 4 minutes per side.
6. In a bowl, mix the cream cheese and ranch seasoning.
7. Spread the cream cheese mixture on top of the chicken.
8. Top with the cheese.
9. Bake in the oven for 10 minutes.
10. Top with the bacon and green onion before serving.

Nutritional Value:

- Calories 743
- Total Fat 48g
- Saturated Fat 20.2g
- Cholesterol 235mg
- Sodium 1523mg
- Total Carbohydrate 4.1g
- Dietary Fiber 0.5g
- Total Sugars 0.8g
- Protein 70.3g
- Potassium 738mg

Creamy Chicken & Mushroom

Preparation Time: 10 minutes
Cooking Time: 20 minutes
Servings: 4

Ingredients:

- 1 lb. chicken tenderloin
- Salt and pepper to taste
- 2 tablespoons butter, divided
- 2 tablespoons olive oil, divided
- ½ lb. mushrooms, sliced
- 2 cloves garlic, crushed
- ¼ cup fresh parsley, chopped
- 2 tablespoons fresh thyme
- 1 cup chicken broth
- ½ cup heavy cream
- ¼ cup sour cream

Method:

1. Season chicken with salt and pepper.
2. Add 1 tablespoon each of butter and olive oil in a pan.
3. Sear the chicken until brown on both sides.
4. Set aside.
5. Add the remaining oil and butter.
6. Cook the mushrooms until crispy.
7. Add the garlic, parsley and thyme.
8. Pour in the broth.
9. Stir in the cream and sour cream.
10. Simmer until the sauce has thickened.
11. Put the chicken back to the sauce.

Nutritional Value:

- *Calories 383*
- *Total Fat 23g*
- *Saturated Fat 10.1g*
- *Cholesterol 122mg*
- *Sodium 611mg*
- *Total Carbohydrate 4.7g*
- *Dietary Fiber 1.2g*
- *Total Sugars 1.3g*
- *Protein 42.1g*
- *Potassium 304mg*

Mozzarella Chicken

Preparation Time: 10 minutes
Cooking Time: 20 minutes
Servings: 4

Ingredients:

- 4 chicken breasts (boneless, skinless)
- 1 tablespoon Italian seasoning, divided
- ½ teaspoon onion powder
- Salt and pepper to taste
- 1 teaspoon paprika
- 1 tablespoon olive oil
- 1 onion, chopped
- 4 cloves garlic, minced
- 1 fire roasted pepper, chopped
- 15 oz. tomato puree
- 2 tablespoons tomato paste
- ¾ cup mozzarella, shredded
- 1 tablespoons parsley, chopped

Method:

1. Preheat your oven to 375 degrees F.
2. Season the chicken with 2 teaspoons Italian seasoning, onion powder, salt, pepper and paprika.
3. Pour the oil in a pan over medium heat.
4. Cook the chicken until brown on both sides.
5. Set aside.
6. Add the onion to the pan.
7. Cook for 3 minutes.
8. Add the garlic and pepper.
9. Cook for 1 minute.
10. Add the tomato puree and tomato paste. Mix well.
11. Stir in the remaining Italian sauce.
12. Simmer for 4 minutes.
13. Arrange the chicken on top of the sauce.
14. Add mozzarella on top.
15. Bake for 2 minutes.
16. Garnish with parsley before serving.

Nutritional Value:

- Calories 387
- Total Fat 16.2g
- Saturated Fat 4.1g
- Cholesterol 130mg
- Sodium 193mg

- Total Carbohydrate 15.8g
- Dietary Fiber 3.3g
- Total Sugars 7.8g
- Protein 44.7g
- Potassium 963mg

Chicken Parmesan

Preparation Time: 20 minutes
Cooking Time: 8 minutes
Servings: 2

Ingredients:

- 2 chicken breast fillets
- 1 tablespoon heavy whipping cream
- 1 egg
- 1 ½ oz. pork rinds, crushed
- 1 oz. Parmesan cheese, grated
- Salt and pepper to taste
- ½ teaspoon garlic powder
- ½ teaspoon Italian seasoning
- 1 tablespoon ghee
- ½ cup tomato sauce
- ¼ cup mozzarella cheese, shredded

Method:

1. Pound chicken fillet until flat.
2. In a bowl, mix the cream and egg.
3. Mix the pork rinds, Parmesan cheese, salt, pepper, garlic powder and Italian seasoning on another plate.
4. Dip the chicken fillet into the egg mixture.
5. Coat with the breading.
6. Add the ghee to a pan over medium heat.
7. Cook the chicken for 3 minutes per side.
8. Put the chicken to a baking pan.
9. Cover the top with tomato sauce and mozzarella cheese.
10. Broil for 2 minutes.

Nutritional Value:

- Calories 589
- Total Fat 33.9g
- Saturated Fat 14.9g
- Cholesterol 282mg
- Total Carbohydrate 5g
- Dietary Fiber 1g
- Total Sugars 3.1g
- Protein 65.3g

Chapter 10: Seafood Recipes

Baked Salmon

Preparation Time: 10 minutes
Cooking Time: 10 minutes
Servings: 4

Ingredients:

- Cooking spray
- 3 cloves garlic, minced
- ¼ cup butter
- 1 teaspoon lemon zest
- 2 tablespoons lemon juice
- 4 salmon fillets
- Salt and pepper to taste
- 2 tablespoons parsley, chopped

Method:

1. Preheat your oven to 425 degrees F.
2. Grease the pan with cooking spray.
3. In a bowl, mix the garlic, butter, lemon zest and lemon juice.
4. Sprinkle salt and pepper on salmon fillets.
5. Drizzle with the lemon butter sauce.
6. Bake in the oven for 12 minutes.
7. Garnish with parsley before serving.

Nutritional Value:

- Calories 345
- Total Fat 22.7g
- Saturated Fat 8.9g
- Cholesterol 109mg
- Sodium 163mg
- Total Carbohydrate 1.2g
- Dietary Fiber 0.2g
- Total Sugars 0.2g
- Protein 34.9g
- Potassium 718mg

Tuna Patties

Preparation Time: 10 minutes
Cooking Time: 10 minutes
Servings: 8

Ingredients:

- 20 oz. canned tuna flakes
- ¼ cup almond flour
- 1 egg, beaten
- 2 tablespoons fresh dill, chopped
- 2 stalks green onion, chopped
- Salt and pepper to taste
- 1 tablespoon lemon zest
- ¼ cup mayonnaise
- 1 tablespoon lemon juice
- 2 tablespoons avocado oil

Method:

1. Combine all the ingredients except avocado oil, lemon juice and avocado oil in a large bowl.
2. Form 8 patties from the mixture.
3. In a pan over medium heat, add the oil.
4. Once the oil starts to sizzle, cook the tuna patties for 3 to 4 minutes per side.
5. Drain each patty on a paper towel.
6. Spread mayo on top and drizzle with lemon juice before serving.

Nutritional Value:

- *Calories 101*
- *Total Fat 4.9g*
- *Saturated Fat 1.2g*
- *Cholesterol 47mg*
- *Sodium 243mg*
- *Total Carbohydrate 3.1g*
- *Dietary Fiber 0.5g*
- *Total Sugars 0.7g*
- *Protein 12.3g*
- *Potassium 60mg*

Grilled Mahi Mahi with Lemon Butter Sauce

Preparation Time: 20 minutes
Cooking Time: 10 minutes
Servings: 6

Ingredients:

- 6 mahi mahi fillets
- Salt and pepper to taste
- 2 tablespoons olive oil
- 6 tablespoons butter
- ¼ onion, minced
- ½ teaspoon garlic, minced
- ¼ cup chicken stock
- 1 tablespoon lemon juice

Method:

1. Preheat your grill to medium heat.
2. Season fish fillets with salt and pepper.
3. Coat both sides with olive oil.
4. Grill for 3 to 4 minutes per side.
5. Place fish on a serving platter.
6. In a pan over medium heat, add the butter and let it melt.
7. Add the onion and sauté for 2 minutes.
8. Add the garlic and cook for 30 seconds.
9. Pour in the chicken stock.
10. Simmer until the stock has been reduced to half.
11. Add the lemon juice.
12. Pour the sauce over the grilled fish fillets.

Nutritional Value:

- Calories 234
- Total Fat 17.2g
- Saturated Fat 8.3g
- Cholesterol 117mg
- Sodium 242mg
- Total Carbohydrate 0.6g
- Dietary Fiber 0.1g
- Total Sugars 0.3g
- Protein 19.1g
- Potassium 385mg

Shrimp Scampi

Preparation Time: 15 minutes
Cooking Time: 10 minutes
Servings: 6

Ingredients:

- 2 tablespoons olive oil
- 2 tablespoons butter
- 1 tablespoon garlic, minced
- ½ cup dry white wine
- ¼ teaspoon red pepper flakes
- Salt and pepper to taste
- 2 lb. large shrimp, peeled and deveined
- ¼ cup fresh parsley, chopped
- 1 teaspoon lemon zest
- 2 tablespoons lemon juice
- 3 cups spaghetti squash, cooked

Method:

1. In a pan over medium heat, add the oil and butter.
2. Cook the garlic for 2 minutes.
3. Pour in the wine.
4. Add the red pepper flakes, salt and pepper.
5. Cook for 2 minutes.
6. Add the shrimp.
7. Cook for 2 to 3 minutes.
8. Remove from the stove.
9. Add the parsley, lemon zest and lemon juice.
10. Serve on top of spaghetti squash.

Nutritional Value:

- Calories 232
- Total Fat 8.9g
- Saturated Fat 3.2g
- Cholesterol 226mg
- Sodium 229mg
- Total Carbohydrate 7.6g
- Dietary Fiber 0.2g
- Total Sugars 0.3g
- Protein 28.9g
- Potassium 104mg

Buttered Cod

Preparation Time: 5 minutes
Cooking Time: 5 minutes
Servings: 4

Ingredients:

- 1 ½ lb. cod fillets, sliced
- 6 tablespoons butter, sliced
- ¼ teaspoon garlic powder
- ¾ teaspoon ground paprika
- Salt and pepper to taste
- Lemon slices
- Chopped parsley

Method:

1. Mix the garlic powder, paprika, salt and pepper in a bowl.
2. Season cod pieces with seasoning mixture.
3. Add 2 tablespoons butter in a pan over medium heat.
4. Let half of the butter melt.
5. Add the cod and cook for 2 minutes per side.
6. Top with the remaining slices of butter.
7. Cook for 3 to 4 minutes.
8. Garnish with parsley and lemon slices before serving.

Nutritional Value:

- Calories 295
- Total Fat 19g
- Saturated Fat 11g
- Cholesterol 128mg
- Sodium 236mg
- Total Carbohydrate 1.5g
- Dietary Fiber 0.7g
- Total Sugars 0.3g
- Protein 30.7g
- Potassium 102mg

Salmon with Red Curry Sauce

Preparation Time: 10 minutes
Cooking Time: 22 minutes
Servings: 4

Ingredients:

- 4 salmon fillets
- 2 tablespoons olive oil
- Salt and pepper to taste
- 1 ½ tablespoons red curry paste
- 1 tablespoon fresh ginger, chopped
- 14 oz. coconut cream
- 1 ½ tablespoons fish sauce

Method:

1. Preheat your oven to 350 degrees F.
2. Cover baking sheet with foil.
3. Brush both sides of salmon fillets with olive oil and season with salt and pepper.
4. Place the salmon fillets on the baking sheet.
5. Bake salmon in the oven for 20 minutes.
6. In a pan over medium heat, mix the curry paste, ginger, coconut cream and fish sauce.
7. Sprinkle with salt and pepper.
8. Simmer for 2 minutes.
9. Pour the sauce over the salmon before serving.

Nutritional Value:

- Calories 553
- Total Fat 43.4g
- Saturated Fat 24.1g
- Cholesterol 78mg
- Sodium 908mg
- Total Carbohydrate 7.9g
- Dietary Fiber 2.4g
- Total Sugars 3.6g
- Protein 37.3g
- Potassium 982mg

Salmon Teriyaki

Preparation Time: 15 minutes
Cooking Time: 25 minutes
Servings: 6

Ingredients:

- 3 tablespoons sesame oil
- 2 teaspoons fish sauce
- 3 tablespoons coconut amino
- 2 teaspoons ginger, grated
- 4 cloves garlic, crushed
- 2 tablespoons xylitol
- 1 tablespoon green lime juice
- 2 teaspoons green lime zest
- Cayenne pepper to taste
- 6 salmon fillets
- 1 teaspoon arrowroot starch
- ¼ cup water
- Sesame seeds

Method:

1. Preheat your oven to 400 degrees F.
2. Combine the sesame oil, fish sauce, coconut amino, ginger, garlic, xylitol, green lime juice, zest and cayenne pepper in a mixing bowl.
3. Create 6 packets using foil.
4. Add half of the marinade in the packets.
5. Add the salmon inside.
6. Place in the baking sheet and cook for about 20 to 25 minutes.
7. Add the remaining sauce in a pan over medium heat.
8. Dissolve arrowroot in water, and add to the sauce.
9. Simmer until the sauce has thickened.
10. Place the salmon on a serving platter and pour the sauce on top.
11. Sprinkle sesame seeds on top before serving.

Nutritional Value:

- Calories 312
- Total Fat 17.9g
- Saturated Fat 2.6g
- Cholesterol 78mg
- Sodium 242mg
- Total Carbohydrate 3.5g

- *Dietary Fiber 0.1g*
- *Total Sugars 0.1g*

- *Protein 34.8g*
- *Potassium 706mg*

Pesto Shrimp with Zucchini Noodles

Preparation Time: 10 minutes
Cooking Time: 15 minutes
Servings: 3

Ingredients:

Pesto sauce

- 3 cups basil leaves
- ¾ cup pine nuts
- 2 cloves garlic
- ½ lemon, juiced
- 1 teaspoon lemon zest
- Salt to taste
- ¼ cup olive oil

Shrimp and Zoodles

- 3 zucchinis
- Salt to taste
- 1 lb. shrimp
- 2 tablespoons avocado oil

Method:

1. Put all the pesto ingredients in a blender.
2. Blend until smooth.
3. Spiralize the zucchini into noodle form.
4. Season with salt.
5. Drain water from the zucchini noodles.
6. Season the shrimp with salt and pepper.
7. Add half of the oil in a pan over medium heat.
8. Once the oil is hot, add the shrimp and cook for 1 to 2 minutes.
9. Add the remaining oil to the pan.
10. Add the zucchini noodles and cook for 3 minutes.
11. Add the pesto and toss to coat the noodles evenly with the sauce.
12. Season with salt.

Nutritional Value:

- Calories 304
- Total Fat 22.2g
- Saturated Fat 2.6g
- Cholesterol 159mg
- Sodium 223mg

- Total Carbohydrate 8g
- Dietary Fiber 2.3g
- Total Sugars 2.5g
- Protein 21.3g
- Potassium 547mg

Crab Cakes

Preparation Time: 1 hour and 20 minutes
Cooking Time: 20 minutes
Servings: 8

Ingredients:

- 2 tablespoons butter
- 2 cloves garlic, minced
- ½ cup bell pepper, chopped
- 1 rib celery, chopped
- 1 shallot, chopped
- Salt and pepper to taste
- 2 tablespoons mayonnaise
- 1 egg, beaten
- 1 teaspoon mustard
- 1 tablespoon Worcestershire sauce
- 1 teaspoon hot sauce
- ½ cup Parmesan cheese, grated
- ½ cup pork rinds, crushed
- 1 lb. crabmeat
- 2 tablespoons olive oil

Method:

1. Add the butter to the pan over medium heat.
2. Add the garlic, bell pepper, celery, shallot, salt and pepper.
3. Cook for 10 minutes.
4. In a bowl, mix the mayo, egg, Worcestershire, mustard and hot sauce.
5. Add the sautéed vegetables to this mixture.
6. Mix well.
7. Add the cheese and pork rind.
8. Fold in the crabmeat.
9. Line the baking sheet with foil.
10. Create patties from the mixture.
11. Place the patties on the baking sheet.
12. Cover the baking sheet with foil.
13. Refrigerate for 1 hour.
14. Fry in olive oil in a pan over medium heat.
15. Cook until crispy and golden brown.

Nutritional Value:

- Calories 150
- Total Fat 9.2g
- Saturated Fat 3.2g
- Cholesterol 43mg
- Sodium 601mg

- Total Carbohydrate 10.8g
- Dietary Fiber 0.5g
- Total Sugars 4.6g
- Protein 6.4g
- Potassium 80mg

Tuna Salad

Preparation Time: 5 minutes
Cooking Time: 0 minute
Servings: 2

Ingredients:

- 1 cup tuna flakes
- 3 tablespoons mayonnaise
- 1 teaspoon onion flakes
- Salt and pepper to taste
- 3 cups Romaine lettuce

Method:

1. Mix the tuna flakes, mayonnaise, onion flakes, salt and pepper in a bowl.
2. Serve with lettuce.

Nutritional Value:

- *Calories 130*
- *Total Fat 7.8g*
- *Saturated Fat 1.1g*
- *Cholesterol 13mg*
- *Sodium 206mg*
- *Total Carbohydrate 8.5g*
- *Dietary Fiber 0.6g*
- *Total Sugars 2.6g*
- *Protein 8.2g*
- *Potassium 132mg*

Chapter 11: Soup and Side Recipes

Coconut Curry Cauliflower Soup

Preparation Time: 10 minutes
Cooking Time: 25 minutes
Servings: 10

Ingredients:

- 2 tablespoons olive oil
- 1 onion, chopped
- 3 tablespoons yellow curry paste
- 2 heads cauliflower, sliced into florets
- 32 oz. vegetable broth
- 1 cup coconut milk
- Minced fresh cilantro

Method:

1. In a pan over medium heat, add the oil.
2. Cook onion for 3 minutes.
3. Stir in the curry paste and cook for 2 minutes.
4. Add the cauliflower florets.
5. Pour in the broth.
6. Increase the heat to high and bring to a boil.
7. Lower the heat to medium.
8. Cook while covered for 20 minutes.
9. Add the coconut milk and cook for an additional minute.
10. Puree in a blender.
11. Garnish with fresh cilantro.

Nutritional Value:

- Calories 138
- Total Fat 11.8g
- Saturated Fat 5.6g
- Sodium 430mg
- Total Carbohydrate 6.4g
- Dietary Fiber 3g
- Total Sugars 2.8g
- Protein 3.6g

Mexican Soup

Preparation Time: 5 minutes
Cooking Time: 15 minutes
Servings: 4

Ingredients:

- 2 teaspoons olive oil
- 1 lb. chicken thighs (skinless and boneless), sliced into smaller pieces
- 1 tablespoon taco seasoning
- 1 cup frozen corn
- 1 cup salsa
- 32 oz. chicken broth

Method:

1. In a pan over medium heat, add oil.
2. Cook chicken for 7 minutes, stirring frequently.
3. Add the taco seasoning and mix well.
4. Add the rest of the ingredients.
5. Bring to a boil.
6. Reduce heat to low and simmer for 5 minutes.
7. Remove fat before serving.

Nutritional Value:

- *Calories 322*
- *Total Fat 12.6g*
- *Saturated Fat 3.1g*
- *Cholesterol 101mg*
- *Sodium 1214mg*
- *Total Carbohydrate 12.2g*
- *Dietary Fiber 2.1g*
- *Total Sugars 3.9g*
- *Protein 39.6g*
- *Potassium 768mg*

Roasted Tomato Soup

Preparation Time: 20 minutes
Cooking Time: 25 minutes
Servings: 6

Ingredients:

- Cooking spray
- 3 ½ lb. tomatoes, sliced into half
- 1 onion, sliced into wedges
- 2 cloves garlic, sliced in half
- 2 tablespoons olive oil
- Salt and pepper to taste
- 2 tablespoons fresh thyme leaves
- 12 fresh basil leaves

Method:

1. Preheat your oven to 400 degrees F.
2. Put the onion, garlic and tomatoes on a baking pan coated with cooking spray.
3. Drizzle vegetables with olive oil and toss.
4. Season with salt, pepper and thyme.
5. Roast for 30 minutes.
6. Place the tomato mixture and basil leaves in a blender.
7. Pulse until smooth.

Nutritional Value:

- Calories 99
- Total Fat 5.3g
- Saturated Fat 0.8g
- Cholesterol 0mg
- Sodium 14mg
- Total Carbohydrate 13g
- Dietary Fiber 4g
- Total Sugars 7.8g
- Protein 2.7g
- Potassium 668mg

Squash Soup

Preparation Time: 15 minutes
Cooking Time: 20 minutes
Servings: 6

Ingredients:

- 5 leeks, sliced
- 2 tablespoons butter
- 4 cups chicken broth
- ¼ teaspoon dried thyme
- 4 cups butternut squash, peeled and cubed
- ¼ teaspoon pepper
- 2 cups cheddar cheese, shredded
- 1 green onion, thinly sliced
- ¼ cup sour cream

Method:

1. In a pan over medium heat, sauté the leeks in butter.
2. Add the broth, thyme, squash and pepper.
3. Bring to a boil and then simmer for 15 minutes.
4. Let it cool.
5. Transfer the mixture to a blender.
6. Pulse until smooth.
7. Stir in the cheese.
8. Garnish with the green onion and sour cream before serving.

Nutritional Value:

- *Calories 320*
- *Total Fat 19.6g*
- *Saturated Fat 11.9g*
- *Cholesterol 54mg*
- *Sodium 794mg*
- *Total Carbohydrate 23.2g*
- *Dietary Fiber 3.3g*
- *Total Sugars 5.7g*
- *Protein 15.1g*
- *Potassium 660mg*

Vegetable Soup

Preparation Time: 5 minutes
Cooking Time: 30 minutes
Servings: 6

Ingredients:

- 2 tablespoons olive oil
- 1 onion, diced
- 2 bell peppers, diced
- 2 cloves garlic, minced
- 2 cups green beans, sliced
- 1 head cauliflower, sliced into florets
- 1 tablespoon Italian seasoning
- 8 cups chicken broth
- 30 oz. diced tomatoes
- Salt and pepper to taste
- 2 dried bay leaves

Method:

1. Pour the olive oil in a pot over medium heat.
2. Sauté the onion and bell peppers for 7 minutes.
3. Add the garlic and cook for 1 minute.
4. Add the rest of the ingredients.
5. Bring to a boil.
6. Reduce to medium low.
7. Simmer for 20 minutes.

Nutritional Value:

- Calories 168
- Total Fat 7.7g
- Saturated Fat 1.4g
- Cholesterol 2mg
- Sodium 1043mg
- Total Carbohydrate 17.1g
- Dietary Fiber 5.1g
- Total Sugars 9.2g
- Protein 9.9g
- Potassium 930mg

Mashed Cauliflower with Chives

Preparation Time: 15 minutes
Cooking Time: 25 minutes
Servings: 4

Ingredients:

- 2 cups chicken broth
- 2 heads cauliflower, cored and sliced into florets
- ¼ cup fresh chives, chopped
- ¼ cup Parmesan cheese, grated
- Salt and pepper to taste

Method:

1. In a pot over medium heat, pour in the chicken broth.
2. Add the cauliflower.
3. Bring to a boil and then simmer for 20 minutes.
4. Transfer cauliflower to a blender.
5. Pulse until smooth.
6. Stir in the chives and cheese.
7. Season with salt and pepper.

Nutritional Value:

- *Calories 98*
- *Total Fat 3.8g*
- *Saturated Fat 2.2g*
- *Cholesterol 10mg*
- *Sodium 551mg*
- *Total Carbohydrate 8.1g*
- *Dietary Fiber 3.4g*
- *Total Sugars 3.6g*
- *Protein 9.6g*
- *Potassium 514mg*

Garlic Parmesan Zucchini

Preparation Time: 5 minutes
Cooking Time: 20 minutes
Servings: 6

Ingredients:

- ¼ cup Parmesan cheese
- ¼ cup mayonnaise
- 1 clove garlic, minced
- Salt to taste
- 2 zucchinis, sliced

Method:

1. Preheat your oven to 400 degrees F.
2. Combine all the ingredients except the zucchini.
3. Spread mixture on top of zucchini.
4. Bake in the oven for 20 minutes.

Nutritional Value:

- *Calories 79*
- *Total Fat 5.4g*
- *Saturated Fat 1.8g*
- *Cholesterol 9mg*
- *Sodium 190mg*
- *Total Carbohydrate 5g*
- *Dietary Fiber 0.7g*
- *Total Sugars 1.8g*
- *Protein 3.9g*
- *Potassium 174mg*

Cheesy Roasted Broccoli

Preparation Time: 5 minutes
Cooking Time: 10 minutes
Servings: 6

Ingredients:

- ¼ cup ranch dressing
- 4 cups broccoli florets
- ¼ cup heavy whipping cream
- ½ cup cheddar cheese, shredded
- Salt and pepper to taste

Method:

1. Preheat your oven to 375 degrees F.
2. Put all the ingredients in a bowl and mix.
3. Arrange the broccoli mix on a baking dish.
4. Bake in the oven for 10 minutes or until tender enough.

Nutritional Value:

- Calories 79
- Total Fat 5.2g
- Saturated Fat 3.1g
- Cholesterol 17mg
- Sodium 137mg
- Total Carbohydrate 4.8g
- Dietary Fiber 1.6g
- Total Sugars 1.4g
- Protein 4.3g
- Potassium 205mg

Stir Fried Green Beans

Preparation Time: 20 minutes
Cooking Time: 10 minutes
Servings: 4

Ingredients:

- 1 lb. green beans, trimmed and sliced
- 2 tablespoons peanut oil
- 2 tablespoons garlic, chopped
- ½ onion, sliced
- Salt to taste
- 1 tablespoon water
- 2 tablespoons oyster sauce

Method:

1. Add peanut oil to a pan over high heat.
2. Heat it for 2 minutes.
3. Add the garlic and onion.
4. Cook for 30 seconds.
5. Add the beans and season with salt.
6. Cook for 2 minutes.
7. Pour in the water and cover the pan.
8. Steam for 5 minutes.
9. Stir in the oyster sauce and cook for 2 minutes.

Nutritional Value:

- Calories 108
- Saturated Fat 1.2g
- Cholesterol 0mg
- Sodium 102mg
- Total Carbohydrate 11g
- Dietary Fiber 4.3g
- Total Sugars 2.2g
- Protein 2.5g
- Potassium 275mg

Roasted Asparagus

Preparation Time: 10 minutes
Cooking Time: 20 minutes
Servings: 4

Ingredients:

- 1 lb. asparagus
- 1 tablespoon peanut oil
- 1 teaspoon coconut oil
- 1 tablespoon soy sauce
- 1 teaspoon sesame oil
- 2 teaspoons sesame seeds

Method:

1. Preheat your oven to 400 degrees F.
2. Arrange the asparagus spears on a baking pan.
3. Brush with peanut oil.
4. Roast for 15 minutes.
5. While waiting, mix the coconut oil, soy sauce and sesame oil.
6. Brush the asparagus with the mixture and roast for 7 minutes.
7. Sprinkle with sesame seeds before serving.

Nutritional Value:

- *Calories 83*
- *Total Fat 6.5g*
- *Saturated Fat 1.9g*
- *Cholesterol 0mg*
- *Sodium 228mg*
- *Total Carbohydrate 5.1g*
- *Dietary Fiber 2.6g*
- *Total Sugars 2.2g*
- *Protein 3g*
- *Potassium 245mg*

Chapter 12: Dessert Recipes

Keto Frosty

Preparation Time: 45 minutes
Cooking Time: 0 minute
Servings: 4

Ingredients:

- 1 ½ cups heavy whipping cream
- 2 tablespoons cocoa powder (unsweetened)
- 3 tablespoons Swerve
- 1 teaspoon pure vanilla extract
- Salt to taste

Method:

1. In a bowl, combine all the ingredients.
2. Use a hand mixer and beat until you see stiff peaks forming.
3. Place the mixture in a Ziploc bag.
4. Freeze for 35 minutes.
5. Serve in bowls or dishes.

Nutritional Value:

- Calories 164
- Total Fat 17g
- Saturated Fat 10.6g
- Cholesterol 62mg
- Sodium 56mg
- Total Carbohydrate 2.9g
- Dietary Fiber 0.8g
- Total Sugars 0.2g
- Protein 1.4g
- Potassium 103mg

Keto Shake

Preparation Time: 15 minutes
Cooking Time: 0 minute
Serving: 1

Ingredients:

- ¾ cup almond milk
- ½ cup ice
- 2 tablespoons almond butter
- 2 tablespoons cocoa powder (unsweetened)
- 2 tablespoons Swerve
- 1 tablespoon chia seeds
- 2 tablespoons hemp seeds
- ½ tablespoon vanilla extract
- Salt to taste

Method:

1. Blend all the ingredients in a food processor.
2. Chill in the refrigerator before serving.

Nutritional Value:

- Calories 104
- Total Fat 9.5g
- Saturated Fat 5.1g
- Cholesterol 0mg
- Sodium 24mg
- Total Carbohydrate 3.6g
- Dietary Fiber 1.4g
- Total Sugars 1.1g
- Protein 2.9g
- Potassium 159mg

Keto Fat Bombs

Preparation Time: 30 minutes
Cooking Time: 0 minute
Servings: 10

Ingredients:

- 8 tablespoons butter
- ¼ cup Swerve
- ½ teaspoon vanilla extract
- Salt to taste
- 2 cups almond flour
- 2/3 cup chocolate chips

Method:

1. In a bowl, beat the butter until fluffy.
2. Stir in the sugar, salt and vanilla.
3. Mix well.
4. Add the almond flour.
5. Fold in the chocolate chips.
6. Cover the bowl with cling wrap and refrigerate for 20 minutes.
7. Create balls from the dough.

Nutritional Value:

- Calories 176
- Total Fat 15.2g
- Saturated Fat 8.4g
- Cholesterol 27mg
- Sodium 92mg
- Total Carbohydrate 12.9g
- Dietary Fiber 1g
- Total Sugars 10.8g
- Protein 2.2g
- Potassium 45mg

Avocado Ice Pops

Preparation Time: 20 minutes
Cooking Time: 0 minute
Servings: 10

Ingredients:

- 3 avocados
- ¼ cup lime juice
- 3 tablespoons Swerve
- ¾ cup coconut milk
- 1 tablespoon coconut oil
- 1 cup keto friendly chocolate

Method:

1. Add all the ingredients except the oil and chocolate in a blender.
2. Blend until smooth.
3. Pour the mixture into the popsicle mold.
4. Freeze overnight.
5. In a bowl, mix oil and chocolate chips.
6. Melt in the microwave. And then let cool.
7. Dunk the avocado popsicles into the chocolate before serving.

Nutritional Value:

- *Calories 176*
- *Total Fat 17.4g*
- *Saturated Fat 7.5g*
- *Cholesterol 0mg*
- *Sodium 6mg*
- *Total Carbohydrate 10.8g*
- *Dietary Fiber 4.5g*
- *Total Sugars 5.4g*
- *Protein 1.6g*
- *Potassium 341mg*

Carrot Balls

Preparation Time: 1 hour and 10 minutes
Cooking Time: 0 minute
Servings: 8

Ingredients:

- 8 oz. block cream cheese
- ¾ cup coconut flour
- ½ teaspoon pure vanilla extract
- 1 teaspoon stevia
- ¼ teaspoon ground nutmeg
- 1 teaspoon cinnamon
- 1 cup carrots, grated
- 1/2 cup pecans, chopped
- 1 cup coconut, shredded

Method:

1. Use a hand mixer to beat the cream cheese, coconut flour, vanilla, stevia, nutmeg and cinnamon.
2. Fold in the carrots and pecans.
3. Form into balls.
4. Refrigerate for 1 hour.
5. Roll into shredded coconut before serving.

Nutritional Value:

- Calories 390
- Total Fat 35g
- Saturated Fat 17g
- Cholesterol 60mg
- Sodium 202mg
- Total Carbohydrate 17.2g
- Dietary Fiber 7.8g
- Total Sugars 6g
- Protein 7.8g
- Potassium 154mg

Coconut Crack Bars

Preparation Time: 2 minutes
Cooking Time: 3 minutes
Servings: 20

Ingredients:

- 3 cups coconut flakes (unsweetened)
- 1 cup coconut oil
- ¼ cup maple syrup

Method:

1. Line a baking sheet with parchment paper.
2. Put coconut in a bowl.
3. Add the oil and syrup.
4. Mix well.
5. Pour the mixture into the pan.
6. Refrigerate until firm.
7. Slice into bars before serving.

Nutritional Value:

- Calories 147
- Total Fat 14.9g
- Saturated Fat 13g
- Cholesterol 0mg
- Sodium 3mg
- Total Carbohydrate 4.5g
- Dietary Fiber 1.1g
- Total Sugars 3.1g
- Protein 0.4g
- Potassium 51mg

Strawberry Ice Cream

Preparation Time: 1 hour and 20 minutes
Cooking Time: 0 minute
Servings: 4

Ingredients:

- 17 oz. coconut milk
- 16 oz. frozen strawberries
- ¾ cup Swerve
- ½ cup fresh strawberries

Method:

1. Put all the ingredients except fresh strawberries in a blender.
2. Pulse until smooth.
3. Put the mixture in an ice cream maker.
4. Use ice cream maker according to directions.
5. Add the fresh strawberries a few minutes before the ice cream is done.
6. Freeze for 1 hour before serving.

Nutritional Value:

- Calories 320
- Total Fat 28.8g
- Saturated Fat 25.5g
- Cholesterol 0mg
- Sodium 18mg
- Total Carbohydrate 25.3g
- Dietary Fiber 5.3g
- Total Sugars 19.1g
- Protein 2.9g
- Potassium 344mg

Key Lime Pudding

Preparation Time: 20 minutes
Cooking Time: 1 hour and 15 minutes
Servings: 2

Ingredients:

- 1 cup hot water
- 2/4 cup erythrytol syrup
- 6 drops stevia
- 1 teaspoon almond extract
- 1 teaspoon vanilla extract
- ¼ teaspoon Xanthan gum powder
- 2 ripe avocados, sliced
- 1 ½ oz. lime juice
- 3 tablespoons coconut oil
- Salt to taste

Method:

1. Add water, erythritol, stevia, almond extract and vanilla extract to a pot.
2. Bring to a boil.
3. Simmer until the syrup has been reduced and has thickened.
4. Turn the heat off.
5. Add the gum powder.
6. Mix until thickened.
7. Add the avocado into a food processor.
8. Add the rest of the ingredients.
9. Pulse until smooth.
10. Place the mixture in ramekins.
11. Refrigerate for 1 hour.
12. Pour the syrup over the pudding before serving.

Nutritional Value:

- Calories 299
- Total Fat 29.8g
- Saturated Fat 12.9g
- Cholesterol 0mg
- Sodium 47mg
- Total Carbohydrate 9.7g
- Dietary Fiber 6.8g
- Total Sugars 0.8g

- Protein 2g

- Potassium 502mg

Conclusion

The ketogenic diet won't achieve worldwide popularity if not for good reason.

It has been proven to be highly effective not only in helping people lose unwanted weight, but also keeping it off, and even improving health in the long run. It can improve skin health, reduce the risk of heart disease and protect your brain from degenerative conditions.

Now the catch is, this diet is quite strict, and therefore requires commitment and consistency.

Without these, you won't achieve success with the ketogenic diet.

So, are you ready to give it a try?

51570519R00061

Made in the USA
Lexington, KY
04 September 2019